# Getting the Sale Handbook

## STUDENT EDITION

From *The Ultimate Toolkit*
www.theultimatetoolkit.com

Jon Spoelstra & Steve DeLay

# GETTING THE SALE HANDBOOK

*The path to becoming a superstar*

Jon Spoelstra & Steve DeLay
December, 2013

# Becoming a superstar in ticket sales

**Welcome.** From this point forward your life will change. You're going to be learning two skills that you will be able to use for the rest of your life. Those two skills are:

1. How to make an appointment with anybody you want to.

2. How to sell a product to the top person in any organization.

These are two exceptionally valuable skills to possess. Less than 1% of Americans possess these skills.

It's not that dfficult to learn this stuff. But, you do have to *precisely* follow the instructions. This means no ad-libbing, no individualizing, no modifying.

After you fully learn these two skills, you may then customize them. However, in the learning process, stay the course that we have set in this booklet.

Have fun. You'll enjoy the ride. You'll really enjoy the benefits.

Jon Spoelstra

Steve DeLay

# *TELLING IS NOT SELLING*

You've made an appointment with the CEO of a local company. Happy times! The appointment is the first step in selling season tickets to a corporation. Now what? What should you say? How should you approach the meeting? That's what I'm going to show you.

What you're reading now—the left column—is me. The right column is what you're supposed to say. As you can see on the right, it's just a big blank space. That's because you're reading right now, not talking.

Before you start to talk, I want to underscore one fundamental in our type of selling.

## Telling is not selling.

Your goal in the meeting is to learn about your prospect's business.

You'll ask a number of questions, but the prospect should speak 70% of the time you are meeting with them. Many young people make the mistake of reversing that percentage. That decreases the possibility of making a sale.

Everything we do in the presentation is to increase the probability of making a sale.

# YOU

*(Blank space means:you're silent)*

# *TYPES OF PRESENTATIONS*

There are basically three types of presentations:

1. **Canned presentation.** This isn't like giving an infomercial where one pitch fits all. While we do have you initially memorize your sales pitch, there are trigger points in the pitch that totally customizes what you're going to recommend to the prospect.

2. **Wing it presentation.** You can't go in to a meeting winging it, without a plan and a thoughtful, detailed strategy. If you choose to wing it, you'll fail most of the time.

3. **Planned presentation.** This is our style. Here's what it is NOT:

   - *Not* a stream of consciousness by the salesperson.
   - *Not* flying blind.
   - *Not* an avalanche of information.

It is a well-orchestrated, well-rehearsed professional presentation.
Our Planned Presentation is a logical, step-by-step process of *teaching* and *learning*.
*You* are *teaching* the prospect how your tickets can be used to increase the prospect's sales.
*You* are *learning* from the prospect which key benefits work best for the prospect's company.

# YOU

*(Blank space over here  means: you're still silent)*

# CONVERSATION

You are going to have a conversation with the prospect on how your team's tickets can improve their business.

Yes, *conversation*.

During your conversation, you are going to tell stories, have pictures and props that will help you make your points.

Think of yourself as a business growth consultant who just happens to recommend your team's tickets as a way for the CEO to help grow their business.

## YOU

*Conversation? Really?*
(You probably thought you were going to
get started on a hyped-up  sales pitch.)

## *3 EASY PARTS*

Your basic presentation should take no more than 10 minutes. Your meeting, however, can last a lot longer because you would be *discussing* different options. But, getting to the point of what you're selling is about ten minutes.

There are three easy parts:

1. **Intro** (takes about 60 seconds).
2. **Pitch** (takes 3-4 minutes).
3. **Close** (takes 4-5 minutes).

Okay, let's get into it. Are you ready?

Yep, now. Let's do it. Go to the next the page.

**YOU**

Now?  Really?

# BREAKING THE PREOCCUPATION BARRIER

When you walk into a prospect's office, that prospect was not thinking about you or your meeting. The prospect was thinking about his/her last phone call or problems at home or which boat to buy.

Trust me, the prospect was *not* thinking about you and your team and how wonderful it would be to buy a bunch of full season tickets.

Thus, you have 30 seconds to get the prospect to consider listening to you and pay attention.

A quick way to catch the prospect's attention is to walk in with a tool of your trade. For instance:

- If you work for a baseball team, walk in carrying a baseball bat.
- If you work for a basketball team, walk in carrying a basketball.
- Hockey? Hockey stick. Or at least a puck.
- Football? Of course, carry in a football.

What's it gonna be?  Hockey stick or baseball bat?  What?

# *WHAT TO SAY AFTER 'HELLO'*

**Stage Direction:** You walk into the prospect's office carrying a tool of your trade (baseball bat, football, etc.).

## *You say:*

⇨⇨⇨⇨⇨⇨⇨⇨⇨⇨⇨⇨⇨⇨⇨⇨⇨⇨⇨⇨⇨⇨⇨⇨⇨⇨⇨⇨⇨⇨⇨⇨⇨⇨⇨⇨⇨⇨⇨⇨⇨⇨

You hand the prospect the prop.

When you hand that bat or basketball or hockey stick to the prospect, you have now successfully broken the preoccupation barrier. You've done it *in seconds*. No longer is that prospect thinking about what he was thinking about before you walked into his office.

I've had a few young salespeople that thought the action was corny. They didn't think it was cool. The purpose of handing over the prop wasn't to be cool; the purpose was to catch the prospect's attention. Using a bat or football or whatever will do that instantaneously.

YOU: "Would you please hold this
while we talk. It's a tool
we use in our business."

## START WITH A QUESTION

Most likely, the prospect will have you sit down in front of his desk.

Once you're seated, you don't start with *small talk*. I know, there are some sales trainers that say you should try to build a bond between the salesperson and the prospect by commenting about something in the prospect's office. Don't even try.

Don't remark about the huge dead fish on the prospect's wall.

Don't comment about the photo of the prospect's family that is on the prospect's desk.

Don't comment about the prospect's university diploma hanging on the wall.

Don't comment on any of that stuff! You're there because the prospect granted you 10 minutes. Don't waste those 10 minutes talking about something else.

With the prospect still holding your baseball bat or hockey stick, **you say in a conversational tone:** ⇨⇨⇨⇨⇨⇨⇨⇨⇨⇨⇨⇨⇨⇨⇨⇨⇨⇨⇨⇨⇨⇨⇨⇨⇨⇨⇨⇨⇨⇨⇨⇨⇨⇨⇨⇨⇨⇨⇨⇨

Bring out an egg of Silly Putty and hold it up. (Again some young salespeople think this is corny, but forget corny, just do it. Silly Putty is one of the most identifiable products worldwide, and you'll see how we use it in the presentation.)

YOU: "We have a thing that
we call silly putty tickets.
Remember silly putty,
you can shape it, stretch it,
mold it.   Well, we can shape
and mold our tickets to
your specific needs to
help you increase your sales."

**(Q.1.)** "For instance, how
many local salespeople
do you have?"

## *YOU ASK YOUR NEXT QUESTION*

*Anything that I put in parenthesis is my notation. You are NOT supposed to say it. Like you're not supposed to say, "Parens Q6 close parens."*

The prospect will answer that first question with a number. 3 or 7 or 1. Whatever. Just remember the number. If the prospect says 'zero' or 'nada', then you'll skip forward through this presentation to the back. But, for the moment, let's say the prospect says "5".

You don't write down the answer to the first question or any of the other questions. That could be a distraction. Just remember the answer. You'll need it later.

**In a conversational tone, ask your second question**:   ⇨⇨⇨⇨⇨⇨⇨⇨⇨⇨⇨⇨⇨⇨⇨⇨

You can put the Silly Putty back in your pocket.

Again, don't write down the answer, but remember it. Like the first answer, you'll refer back to the second answer later on.

- 5 accounts
- 5 sales people

**(Q.2.)** "How many key accounts does each salesperson have?"

**In a conversational tone, ask your third question**:

Let's say the prospect answers $25,000 or whatever, the size of a key account.  Yep, you guessed it, don't write down the answer, but remember it.

Four questions asked, only two more to go.

**In a conversational tone, ask your fourth and fifth  question:** ⇨⇨⇨⇨⇨⇨⇨⇨⇨⇨⇨

**(Q.3.)** "What size is
an important account?"

**(Q.4.)** "How important is new
business to your salespeople?"

**(Q.5.)** "Do you have a strict
plan that is designed to get
new business every month?"

That's it! You just accomplished your intro in 60 seconds or less! And, you got some valuable information from the prospect that will allow you to custom fit your presentation.

This was pretty easy, eh? Just asking these five questions. With answers, it will take less than 60 seconds.

**Q1.** How many local sales people do you have?

**Q2**. How many key accounts does each salesperson have?

**Q3**. What size is an important account?

**Q4**. How important is new business to your salespeople?

**Q5**. Do you have a strict plan that is designed to get new business every month?"

## *HOORAY, THAT'S THE END OF PART 1, THE INTRO!*

# Part 2: The Pitch

**In a conversational tone, you say:** ⇨⇨⇨⇨⇨⇨⇨⇨⇨⇨⇨⇨⇨⇨⇨

Most likely, the answer to Question #6 will be, "No, that's not a problem."

**Continuing on in a conversational tone, you say:**
⇨⇨⇨⇨⇨⇨⇨⇨⇨⇨⇨⇨⇨⇨⇨⇨⇨⇨

"It's always tough to get salespeople to focus on new business. By using our silly putty tickets, you can get them to *focus on new business,* and *you can keep track.* For example, the first step is to have each salesperson identify in writing to you which new prospects are key to them."

**(Q.6.)** "That wouldn't be Difficult to do, would it?"

"Most of my clients have told me the key to building business from new prospects is for the salesperson to develop a good relationship with them, usually through constant contact."

**Continuing on in a conversational tone, you say:** ⇨⇨⇨⇨⇨⇨⇨⇨⇨⇨⇨⇨⇨⇨⇨

"A lot of times, to build that relationship, salespeople will use an out-of-the-office activity like golf or lunches."

"Some of my clients have told me their problem with golf is that some people just may not be good golfers and it's almost more embarrassing to playthan not. And, it's pretty expensive. And when was the last time you had a memorable chicken sandwich at lunch?"

"However, by using our Silly Putty tickets, you can get them to build these relationships and focus on new business, and you can keep track."

I just made up the Kangaroo name.  Obviously, you're supposed to use your own team's name.

"Here's how it works. The salesperson calls a prospect who he has been working on for a little while. He says, 'How about joining me for the **Kangaroos** game next week. I've got the president's seats.'

"This is <u>not</u> a situation of the salesperson just giving away the seats--it's the salesperson *inviting* the prospect *to go with him*.
Now, the salesperson has the chance to do some real out-of-the-office bonding."

"Remember, he wants to develop a relationship through constant contact. Giving the tickets away doesn't help build that relationship."

**Q7** is a critical question. The prospect usually answers in a positive manner. But what if the prospect gives a **<u>negative answer</u>** saying, "I'm not sure that going to a game would help in building a relationship..." or something like that.

You need to dig deeper on a negative answer or objection. **To do that you would ask:**
⇨⇨⇨⇨⇨⇨⇨⇨⇨⇨⇨⇨⇨⇨⇨⇨⇨⇨⇨⇨⇨⇨⇨⇨⇨⇨⇨⇨⇨⇨⇨⇨⇨

Whatever the prospect says, listen and then bring out an **Evidence Letter**. An 'Evidence Letter' is a letter from a local company extolling the business values of having tickets to your games. Your Sales Manager will provide you with several Evidence Letters.

**(Q.7.)** "How effective do you think 2-3 hours at one of our Kangaroo games would be for building a relationship?"

CEO: (Says something, positive or negative)

"How do you mean?"

"Other companies thought that too, but look at one of my clients who enjoyed success with our tickets..."

You should be ready with a testimonial letter/email regardless of whether the CEO says *yes* or *no* to Question 8. You should have 3-4 testimonial letters at your fingertips in your bag. Don't put them in a plastic sheath as that will make them look too contrived. Also, highlight the key phrases and areas of the letter that show the benefits the client received. You want the CEO to take the letter and read those particular points.

**Continuing in a conversational tone, you say:** ⇨⇨⇨⇨⇨⇨⇨⇨⇨⇨⇨⇨⇨⇨⇨⇨⇨⇨⇨

As you ask question #9, lean forward in your seat a little bit and hold up your right hand with the index finger extended. This is to emphasize that it's only <u>one</u> night a month out of 30 nights. This is a critical question that you have to get a *yes* answer to. If the CEO says the salespeople could go one day a month, it eliminates a potential future objection of "*I'm not sure my salespeople will use the tickets.*" It's vital that the CEO answers this question. Don't answer it for them.

"You're exactly right, look at one of my clients who has enjoyed success with our tickets ... "

(**Stage direction**: *Hand the prospect one of your Evidence Letters*.)
"What could be even better when taking a prospect to a game is if you, as the president, or maybe your sales manager could go also."

(**Q.8.**)  "Would you be willing to do that occasionally for the right account?"


(**Q.9.**)  "Would it be asking too much of your salespeople to spend just one evening a month with a key prospect at one of our games?"

**Q.10** is really a key question. Usually you'll get an answer with a number. *Any* number is OK, but you need a number. If the prospect says, "I don't know," then you'll go with the minimum number, *one*.

This is how the math would look:

"If each salesperson converted *just one* prospect to become a new customer that would be $25,000 (remember, that was the prospect's answer to (Q3) for each salesperson. With 5 salespeople (remember, that was the prospect's answer to (Q1),that would be $125,000 in new business."

You could expand that by adding, "What if each salesperson converted *2 prospects* into customers? That would bring you $250,000 in *new* business."

"Our season is about six months long. If each one of your salespeople took *just one keyprospect a month to one of our games,* each salesperson would bring six new prospects a season."

**(Q.10**.) "Of those six prospects, how many do you think would end up as *customers?*"

"If each salesperson converted just one prospect to become a new customer, that would be $_____ (the avg. size of an important account from Q3) for each salesperson. With _____ (enter the number of salespeople from Q1) salespeople, that would be $_____ in new business (multiply the average size of an account by the number of local salespeople)."

While this may seem like a simplistic question, you need to make sure the CEO understands your math. If there's confusion, your chances of a sale plummet.

Having him say *yes* means you have the revenue side of the return on investment.

You might have to explain like this: "Well, you told me that you have 5 local salespeople and the average key account is $25,000. Assuming the salespeople would only convert one of the six prospects to become a new customer, I multiplied 5 times $25,000 to come up with the $125,000 in new business."

**(Q.11.)** "Do you see how I arrived at this number?"

**Continuing in a conversational tone, you say:** ⇨⇨⇨⇨⇨⇨⇨⇨⇨⇨⇨⇨⇨⇨⇨⇨⇨⇨⇨⇨⇨⇨

The CEO will most likely agree and say something like, "*They better, that's part of their job.*"

"You know, we've been talking about new business. We might also consider your existing clients. After all, your competitor may be out there trying to build the same relationships with your clients."

**(Q.12.)** "Would it be asking too much to have your salespeople also spend just one evening with an existing
client as well as one evening with a prospect?"

The math here is easy. 5 salespeople each going to one game per month equals five games a month.

Same math. 5 x 1 = 5 games.

Adding the games for new prospects (5) to the games for existing business (5) equals 10 games. You'll notice, we've been focusing on games per month. That is generally easier for a prospect to accept as opposed to the total number of games. For instance, 10 games per month doesn't sound as imposing as MLB's 81 games or NBA's 41 games for a full season.

**Continuing in a conversational tone, you say:** ⇨⇨⇨⇨⇨⇨⇨⇨⇨⇨⇨⇨⇨

You should be recommending a *specific* ticket package and seating location. This is not a gallery of different ticket packages. You should have plenty of pictures of the seating area you are recommending. You should also have a one-page document on the benefits and amenities for your recommendation.

Get animated. Move to the edge of your seat and start using your hands more. This is where you have to show excitement for your product.

"To give each salesperson one game a month to take out a *prospect*, you would need _____ games a month."

**(Q.13.)** <u>"Does that make sense to you?"</u>

"You would need a similar amount of games per month
for your salespeople to take *existing* clients out to the
games. You would also need _____ games per month. You need a total of _____ games per month.

## *THAT'S IT, THAT'S YOUR PITCH*

Our sales pitch is probably nothing close to what you imagined.

You can see where we believe you are more of a consultant than a salesperson. You're trying to find *the right ticket package for the prospect*, not trying to jam something they can't use down their throats.

To see how you close this out, turn the page to see The Close.

"Now let's talk about which type of ticket package would work best for you."

"Based on what you've told me, here's what I would suggest you do.

"Our best seating area is the Club Level.  With these seats, here is what you get…"

(*Outline the benefits of the Club Level seats.*)

# Part 3: The Close

# CLOSING TOOL

| Sales people | Prospects | Clients | G | # of pkgs | Comments | Best Ticket Cost | Next Best Ticket Cost |
|---|---|---|---|---|---|---|---|
| 2 | 6 | 6 | 24 | 4 20-games | 4 fewer prospects or clients | $3,600 | $2,160 |
| 3 | 6 | 6 | 36 | 4 40-games | 4 games for employees, clients | $7,200 | $4,320 |
| 4 | 6 | 6 | 48 | 4 40-games | 8 fewer prospects | $7,200 | $4,320 |
| 5 | 6 | 6 | 60 | 4 81-games | 21 games for employees, clients | $14,000 | $8,640 |
| 6 | 6 | 6 | 72 | 4 81-games | 9 games for employees, clients | $14,000 | $8,640 |
| 7 | 6 | 6 | 84 | 4 81-games | 3 fewer prospects | $14,000 | $8,640 |
| 8 | 6 | 6 | 96 | 4 81-games; 4 20s | 5 games for employees more clients | $17,600 | $10,560 |
| 9 | 6 | 6 | 108 | 4 81-games; 4 20s | 7 fewer prospects/clients | $17,600 | $10,560 |
| 10 | 6 | 6 | 120 | 4 81-games; 4 40s | 1 fewer prospects/clients | $17,600 | $10,560 |

(**Stage Direction**: You can use the Closing Tool Chart on the left to help you close. I used to print these on 3.4" x 8" card that I would carry in my inside suit jacket pocket.)

**Chart Layout**
Column 1: Number of local salespeople.
Column 2: Each salesperson needs tickets for 6 prospects (one game per month).
Column 3. Each salesperson *might* need tickets for 6 current accounts (one game per month).
Column 4. Total games needed for this prospect.
Column 5. Best ticket package for that need. (If you had an 81 game home schedule)
Column 6. How those tickets can be used.
Column 7, 8. Prices for four tickets per ticket package needed.

"The cost to have a planned, controlled, new business effort is really quite nominal for the return.  For each one of your salespeople to take just one key prospect once a month and one current client a month,you would need _____ games per month or _____ games for the season."

*(**Stage instruction**: In our example, 5 salespeople would need 10 games per month or 60 games for the season. You should have a chart like the one on the left.   Look at your chart and find the row with 5 salespeople.  You don't have to stumble around doing math, it's right there.)*

"The return on investment is substantial.   If each salesperson brought in only one new piece of new business because of this focus on new business, your sales would increase to $125,000." ($25,000 x 5 = $125,000) Because you need 60 games, I recommend four full season tickets.  That would leave 21 games for your employees or more customers.  Your costs for 4 season tickets is only $14,000. How happy do you think you'd be with those results by giving this plan a try?

## *FIRST TIME*

With **Q14**, this would be the first time you're asking for the order. Instead of asking a yes/no question, you're asking a question that the prospect has to answer affirmatively or with an objection.

That decision would be worth at least $125,000 in new business to you and maybe up to $250,000 in new business."

"I can get this order in today and reserve you some prime seats."

**(Q.14.)** <u>"Would you prefer the account in your name or the company's name?"</u>

**(Stage instruction: PAUSE --- BE SILENT after asking Question 14. I'm also going to call a TIME OUT right now to briefly talk to you about handling objections. See my comments in the column to the left.)**

With Question 14, you'll get one of these three results:

1. **The order**. Terrific, write it up.

2. **Questions.** These aren't necessarily objections, but more like something you need to clarify.

   - **Objections.** Objections are part of the sales process. You are pretty certain to get at least one or two objections. Here are a few keys to keep in mind when facing objections:

   - *Pause.* When you hear an objection, pause for 3-4 seconds even if it is your favorite objection to answer. It makes the prospect feel that you are deeply considering their concerns.

   - *"How do you mean?"* This is my all-time favorite initial response to any objection. The purpose of asking this question is to get the prospect to expand on their concern. The more information you have surrounding the objection, the easier it will be to respond to it and overcome it.

   - *Be understanding.* Your prospect gave you an objection they believe is real. If you argue with them, or tell them that their objection is without any merit, the prospect will feel you aren't listening. That's a quick recipe for "No Sale." Use the Feel, Felt, Found method to make them believe you are receptive to their problem.

     "I can understand why you might *feel* that way. I have had a couple of other clients who initially *felt* the same way. Here's what they *found* after using this program for a season or two." Hand the prospect a testimonial letter that illustrates

(**Stage instruction**:  I'm a little long winded here, but catch your breath and get ready to push the close in a socially acceptable manner.)

someone who was a skeptic initially but has come around to having tremendous success with your team's tickets.

- *Get it down to one objection.* Prospects will many times throw up smokescreen objections. You need to root out all those smokescreens and find the real objection. This can be done by asking simply, "Other than _____ (insert the original objection), is there anything else preventing you from buying?"

- *Avoid a follow-up phone call as the next step.* In the cases where you don't get a *yes* or *no* on the spot, the prospect may tell the salesperson to call them back in a few days/weeks. That's just a way of politely brushing them off without having to say *no* to their face. The prospect will just not answer the phone or return calls in the future whenever the salesperson tries to follow up. Instead, push for a follow-up meeting.

Silence is your strongest closing tool. The most difficult part of *selling* is asking for the order. The most difficult part of closing a sale is *not talking your way out of a sale*. Let the silence do the closing for you.

# Handling Objections

## *FOOTNOTES TO PARTNER OBJECTION*

1.  It's important to flush out a specific time that the CEO plans to meet with his partner to discuss your ticket package.

2.  Asking what their recommendation is puts the CEO on the spot. If he says, "*I'm just going to give it to him and see what he thinks*," that means the CEO really isn't enthusiastic about your program. You should remind the prospect of the previous recommendation he agreed with and make sure that's what is going to be recommended. Reluctance to do that most likely means there is another hidden objection that needs to be flushed out.

3.  I like to use the word 'inclined' here. If you just ask, "What do you think your partner will say?" you open the door for the prospect to say, "*I don't know. That's why I have to ask.*" By using the word '*inclined*' the prospect has to make a guess at what his partner will say.

4.  If he does give an objection, the salesperson has to learn why the partner would hesitate. Asking this question helps flush out what the partner's objection could be.

5.  The Opt-Out Clause is a strategy we have used with various teams. There is no risk to the prospect with the Opt-Out Clause. If they balk at this offer, there is some other objection holding them back.

## LET ME TALK TO MY PARTNER (or talk to someone else) Objection

CEO: "It sounds pretty good. Let me talk to my partner (wife or business manager or pet dog or whatever) and get back to you on this."

YOU: "I can understand wanting to talk to your partner. When do you think you'll talk to your partner?"[1]

**(Stage instruction: When you see a footnote number, check my tip on the opposite page.)**

CEO: "Thursday (or whatever specific date)."

YOU: "Having looked at this program and looked at the new business potential, what will your recommendation be?" [2]

CEO: (see footnote #2)

YOU: "What do you think your partner would be <u>inclined</u> to say?" [3]

CEO: "I think he'd like it." (If the CEO gives you an objection here, ask "How do you mean?") [4]

YOU: "Then why don't we do this. Let's sign you up today and we'll use our Opt-Out Clause [5]. Here's how it works. You're meeting with your partner on Thursday (see above).

"Well, I'll write next Monday's date at the top of the agreement. You have until that date to Opt-Out if you decide that this isn't for you. This way, you can get better seat locations, but if you and your partner decide that this isn't for you by next Monday, you just call me up and I'll cancel the order."

CEO: "I'm not sure. I really need to talk to him."

YOU: "We can still do the Opt-Out. When you meet with your partner on Thursday (see above), and your partner doesn't like the $_____ in new revenue for a cost of $_____, then just call me and I'll cancel the deal."

# PART 3: THE CLOSE, HANDLING OBJECTIONS
## FOOTNOTES SALESPEOPLE OBJECTION

1. We're trying to get generalities out of the equation and get a specific timeframe. You might need this specific timeframe a little later.

2. This was the answer to Q9. Now you can see why you had to ask Q9 earlier or this is an easy objection for the prospect to use. Since the CEO earlier said *yes* to Q9, all the salesperson is doing here is simply reminding him that earlier he thought the salespeople could use the tickets.

3. Earlier, the CEO agreed in Q7 that Big City Kangaroos were a good place to build relationships. And, in Q10 and Q11, he agreed on the amount of new business that could be generated in the plan. Again, you're simply reminding him of those answers.

CEO: "Looks pretty good. Let me talk to my salespeople and make sure they are into it and get back to you."

YOU: "When would you talk to your salespeople about this?" [1]

CEO: "Thursday."

YOU: "Jim, you said earlier that it wouldn't be too much to ask of your salespeople to spend one night a month out with a key prospect, right?" [2]

CEO: "I think it's reasonable."

YOU: "And, you said you thought Big City Kangaroos' games were a good place to develop relationships and there was a potential of _____ in new business, right?" [3]

CEO: "Sure."

YOU: "Then with all due respect to your salespeople, why let them even vote on it? Why let them vote on $125,000 of new revenue for your company? If you think this will work and you think they can spend just one evening a month out with a prospect, and generate $125,000 to $250,000 in new business, what's there to vote on? *What if they*

# PART 3: THE CLOSE, HANDLING OBJECTIONS
## FOOTNOTES SALESPEOPLE OBJECTION

4.  Like in the "Let me talk to my partner" objection, the Opt-Out Clause offer is positioned to remove every hurdle from the prospect buying. If the CEO says no to the opt-out option, he is not convinced that Big City Kangaroos' tickets will help improve his business.

5.  Silence is the most powerful closing tool. Don't talk yourself out of a sale. Let the prospect speak next

*voted no?* I had a client last year who was concerned about whether his salespeople would use the tickets. Here's how well it worked for him."

**(STAGE DIRECTIONS: Hand a testimonial letter to the CEO.)**

YOU: (when CEO looks up from the letter.) "Why don't we do this? Let's sign you up today and we'll use our Opt-Out Clause [4].

Here's how it works. You're meeting with your salespeople on Thursday (see above). Well, I'll write next Monday's date at the top of the agreement. You have until that date to Opt-Out if you decide that this isn't for you. This way, you can get better seat locations, but if your sales staff really fights you on this, by next Monday, just call me up and I'll cancel the order. Can I reserve those seats today?"

BE SILENT AND LET THE PROSPECT SPEAK NEXT [5]

**NOTE: Here's a terrific example of why sellouts matter so much. Seat location is the primary reason to get someone to sign up on the spot, particularly for the big games.**

# PART 3: THE CLOSE, HANDLING OBJECTIONS

## FOOTNOTES ON COST TOO MUCH OBJECTION

1.    This is a very important question to ask for the cost objection.  You need the prospect to tell you why the cost is an issue.  Is it the payment structure, budget, or just the overall cost?  You should have payment plan options to overcome most objections.  If it's the overall cost, you need them to give you a number that works for them so you aren't selling against yourself.

2.    You have reminded the prospect of everything that has been discussed and how successful the program could be.  The cost issue may be a smokescreen.  By asking what else is really causing them to hesitate (not say *no*, just hesitate), you are trying to flush out the most important objection.

| COST TOO MUCH objection |
| --- |

CEO: "I like the concept, but it costs too much."

YOU: "How do you mean?" [1]

CEO: "Well, we've had a tough year and cut some budgets so I have to be smart on expenses" (or some other expanded explanation).

YOU: "I can understand that. (pause) You know, think about it this way. You said yourself that you thought you could generate $ _____ in new business for a pretty
reasonable cost of $ _____. That sounds like a pretty smart move on your part. What is it here that is really causing you to hesitate?" [2]

# PART 3: THE CLOSE, HANDLING OBJECTIONS

## FOOTNOTES ON COST TOO MUCH OBJECTION

3.    I can't emphasize this enough. That's why I've put it in ALL CAPS, bold letters. Consider that I'm SHOUTING. Silence is the most powerful closing tool you have.

4.    Whatever number the prospect gives you should be the minimum order you receive. By giving you a number, they are in essence telling you, "This is what I can buy." Now just adjust the package to get at least that amount.

## COST TOO MUCH objection (con't)

BE SILENT AND LET THE PROSPECT SPEAK NEXT [3]

**(STAGE DIRECTIONS: If the prospect really continues to persist that it is indeed a cost issue, you don't want to become pushy. It's okay to downsell them to make them more comfortable with the purchase. Your goal is to make a sale.)**

YOU: "What would you be more comfortable with?" [4]

**(STAGE DIRECTIONS: Whatever figure he gives you, it's probably the low figure. Come up with a package that is lower than your original figure but a little higher than his second number.)**

YOU: "Within that price range, I think this could work for you. (cut the original recommendation down with either a cheaper priced ticket or fewer games)
.
YOU: "With this plan, you can still get really good seat locations and pretty close to the right number of games. If this works the way we both think it will, you can always add games or upgrade your seats during the season. Will this work for you?"
BE SILENT AND LET THE PROSPECT SPEAK NEXT

# PART 3: THE CLOSE, HANDLING OBJECTIONS

## FOOTNOTES ON CLIENTS NOT LIKING SPORTS

1.      This is usually a smokescreen objection.  Unless the CEO has a real limited number of clients in the market, they have to have fans of the sport or team. You need to dig deep to find out the real objection.

YOU: "How do you mean?"

CEO: (Some additional explanation[1])

YOU: "That makes sense to think about your clients. Let's really think about this though. This program really is designed to get *new* business. You said earlier that our games would be an effective place to build relationships, right? Well, prospects might not be fans of our team, but most like to see the biggest stars of the league at some of our biggest and best sold out games. This works for getting new business and it will work for most of your clients.
I can take your order right now and get this new business program going."

**BE SILENT AND LET THE PROSPECT SPEAK NEXT**

# PART 3: THE CLOSE, HANDLING OBJECTIONS

## FOOTNOTES ON JUST BEST GAMES

1. Most business executives think of StubHub as an easy solution to save some money. They most likely have never actually bought anything from Stub Hub and don't know the hurdles. It's important to point them out. Most likely, anyone suggesting they will buy from StubHub doesn't really believe that the ticket program you have recommended will actually work.

2. This is the biggest weakness of StubHub. The idea of owning season tickets allows the prospect to *plan* for developing relationships. Purchasing from StubHub means the company is not planning ahead. The prospect would only be reacting to a client or prospect requesting tickets.

3. Getting the real concern out in the open is the only way you'll successfully overcome both of these objections.

## I'll JUST BUY THE GOOD GAMES
## FROM STUB HUB Objection

CEO: "I'll just buy the good games from Stub Hub."

YOU: "I can understand how easy it is to buy from StubHub. However, StubHub has some weaknesses for businesses: [1] You can't really plan in advance with a controlled new business strategy. [2] You never really know how much you'll pay for tickets and more importantly, whether you can get decent seats.

YOU: "You also don't get access to the other features and benefits of being a ticket package buyer with the team. What is it that is really causing you to hesitate here?" [3]

# PART 3: THE CLOSE, HANDLING OBJECTIONS

## FOOTNOTES ON WORKING OBJECTION

1. I'm using the sample scenario that we have laid out. Obviously, you would put in the numbers that are appropriate to the CEO that you're meeting with.

CEO: "I just can't see this working..."

YOU: "I can understand that this sounds crazy that you can get all this new business by going to games. But, IT DOES WORK. And, what is your risk? It's only about $14,000[1]. That's not much of a gamble—$14,000 to get $125,000, maybe $250,000. What if it isn't as effective as I say it is? What if it's only 75% effective?

That would mean you would get over $90,000 in new business for a $14,000 investment. Plus you'll have a lot of fun at our games. Would it be all right if I placed your order today?"

# PART 3: THE CLOSE, HANDLING OBJECTIONS

## FOOTNOTES ON THINKING ABOUT IT OBJECTION

1. Most of us use the 'I'd like to think about' objection in personal and business situations. When do we use it? It's when we're not enthusiastically sure of doing something. So, this is a normal reaction. We need to reiterate the good reasons for doing something.

2. I like the word *inclined* in this situation. You're almost putting the prospect into the third person. *Inclined* isn't making a decision, it's *leaning* one specific way.

3. If they're *inclined* to do it, they might just need a *nudge*. This is the nudge.

CEO: "I'd like to think about it." [1]

YOU: "I can understand that. If you took some time to think about it—maybe even thinking about it walking some beach—and you thought about the $_____ in new sales and the $_____ in cost, do you think you would be *inclined* [2] to do it?"

(If the answer is **yes** or **probably**, say, "Well, then, why don't we just do it. You'll really be pleased with the results.") [3]

(If the answer is **no** or **probably not**, ask why. "Really? You'd be getting $_____ in new revenue and it cost only $_____. What is it that's really causing you to hesitate here?")

(You'll probably get a real objection. Now you can handle the objection directly.)

# PART 3: THE CLOSE, HANDLING OBJECTIONS

## FOOTNOTES ON HESITATING

1. You don't have to wait for the CEO to hesitate to use another Endorsement Letter. You should be carrying five or six Endorsement Letters. An Endorsement Letter is good when the action slows down in the case of hesitation. Just handing the letter to the CEO creates movement and helps get the CEO thinking about the positive elements of your ticket package.

## TO THOSE WHO HESITATE

CEO: (Hesitating)

YOU: "Let me tell you about a CEO that was in the same position as you and he followed this plan and decided to give it a try.  Take a look at these numbers..."

**(Hand the prospect another Endorsement Letter [1] and be quiet while the CEO reads it.)**

YOU:  "How happy do you think he is that he gave this plan a try?  That decision was worth $100,000 in new business to him.  Let me get this order in today.  Don't worry about a thing, I'll take care of all the details..."

# PART 3: THE CLOSE & MAKING THE DECISION

| PROS | CONS |
|---|---|
| | |

1. $125,000

2. Renewal of year 1 business

Equals $100,000 over next year.

3. Total increase in new business:

$225,000

## FOOTNOTES ON MAKING THE DECISION

1. You're fishing, of course, for problematic objections. You don't mind having to put down one or two more objections.

## MAKING THE DECISION

**(Stage direction:  You can use this anytime while handling objections.)**

YOU:  "Let's take a look at this….the pros and the cons.

(Take out a blank piece of paper for this.  Draw a line vertically down the middle.  Write 'Pros' in the upper left [1] and 'Cons' in the upper right.)[1]

Let's put down the amount of new business in the left hand column..."

**(Stage direction:  hand write the new business number on your chart.)**

# PART 3: THE CLOSE & MAKING THE DECISION

2. Let's say the prospect says that they would renew about 80%. That would be an additional $100,000 of revenue next year even if they didn't buy tickets again. So, the total increase for new business from that ticket package would be $225,000.

| PROS | CONS |
| --- | --- |
| 1. $125,000 | 1. $14,400 |
| 2. Renewal of year 1 business | 2. Effectiveness?? |

Equals $100,000 over next year.

   3. Total increase in new business:

$225,000

   2. Yes, you're fishing for objections! We're looking for that hidden objection that could kill a sale. If you find that hidden objection, you increase your chances for a sale.

3. I threw a soft ball here with an easy objection. But, once you learn this stuff, you're prepared to effectively respond to any objective.

YOU: "Of that new business you would get, is it business that you can *renew*? If so, what percent do you think you could renew?" (2)

**(Stage direction: based on the answer, hand write that number on your chart.)**

YOU: "That's $225,000 in new business and that's if your salespeople convert only one in six of their prospects. Now let's look at the Cons."

**(Stage direction: hand write the word Cons in the right hand column.)**

YOU: "What would be the first 'reason against'?"

YOU: "You might say expense. Let me write down $14,400."

**(Stage direction: hand write the cost of the ticket package you're recommending.)**

YOU: "Anything else?" (2)

CEO: "I don't know how effective this would be." (3)

**(Stage direction: hand write that objection onto the Reasons Against column. You then handle that objection like we have outlined in this Handbook.)**

YOU: "Let's take a look at this. It looks like a pretty easy decision. You get $225,000 in new revenue at a cost of $14,000. Let me get your order in today…"

# PART 3: THE CLOSE

1. Rookie salespeople are usually just happy to leave the prospect on their 'pending' list and avoid an immediate *no*. They just want to get out of that meeting unscathed. A 'maybe' or a 'call me back in a week' feels like a victory, but unfortunately it usually isn't. Get the second meeting!

2. The salesperson may not really have a follow-up meeting at that time, but it's important for the CEO to think he does. This way, it doesn't seem like the salesperson is making a special trip which the CEO could ask him not to do. By asking for the time slot ahead of the previously scheduled meeting, the salesperson makes the CEO feel like it will be a short, quick meeting.

3. If the CEO hems and haws and doesn't want to schedule a follow-up meeting, that's a warning sign. They know they can dodge a phone call, but a meeting will force them to make a yes/no decision. Most people don't like to give a *no* answer in a face-to-face meeting. They prefer to avoid conflicts.

4. Repeat the time of the meeting and go through the action of actually putting the appointment in your phone or your appointment book. This way, the CEO sees you doing it and feels obligated to put it on his own calendar. It makes it harder for the CEO to skip out on the follow-up meeting. When the salesperson returns to the office, he should send the CEO an official meeting notice for the follow-up appointment so there is no chance it will get missed or ignored.

| GETTING THE FOLLOW-UP MEETING |
|---|

**(STAGE DIRECTIONS:** Every meeting doesn't end in a yes or no answer. There are times when follow up is needed. You should never settle for a follow-up phone call. Usually that ends up becoming a lot of chasing of the CEO to get a final yes or no answer. It's better to get the follow-up meeting when you're already meeting with the CEO[1]. Getting the follow-up meeting could go like this.)

CEO: "I'm not sure about this and have to talk to a few people first. Give me a call next week and I'll let you know."

YOU: "I can understand that. I am actually going to be right down the street at _____ (insert company) for a meeting at 10:00am on Tuesday. Would it be okay to stop by here at 9:30am to answer any new questions or get this wrapped up?" [2]

**(STAGE DIRECTIONS:** The salesperson should be reaching in to their bag for an appointment book or their cell phone for a calendar. This will make it seem more 'official' that they are going to be back in the area.)

CEO: (will give you a yes/no answer or another date) [3]

**STAGE DIRECTIONS: Once the CEO says *yes*, the salesperson should mark the date down on either their phone calendar or in their appointment book. Don't just write it on a sheet of paper.)**

YOU: "Great, I've got down that I will see you next Tuesday at 9:30am. Does that work for you?" [4]

# CHANGE OF DIRECTION

## Notes on the Questions for Group Sales

**Q1.** You've come to a fork in the road when you ask how many local salespeople the company has and the answer is *zero*. This whole pitch is based on using our tickets to help a company improve its sales, and they do that with local salespeople. Without any local salespeople, the company really doesn't have a reason to buy season tickets. However, they do indeed have a reason to buy tickets—*Group Tickets*.

If a company bought 200 tickets from an NBA team for a group outing, that would translate to five full season tickets. So, when a CEO says they have no local salespeople we still look at it as an opportunity to sell a bunch of tickets.

**Q2.** It's important to know the size of the company. The more employees the better.

**Q3.** This question gives a better idea of the CEO's philosophy on employee reward and recognition. If they do none, it's going to be tough to sell him on using tickets for employee reward and recognition. If they are active, the chance of a sale goes up dramatically.

**Q4.** This helps define the regularity of employee reward and recognition. Infrequent recognition would likely lead the salesperson to recommend a larger, hospitality-style event. Frequent recognition would drive the recommendation more toward a ticket package.

# WHAT IF THEY DON'T HAVE
# ANY LOCAL SALESPEOPLE?

**Q1.** "How many local salespeople do you have?" That was the first question of this presentation. What happens when the prospect says *zero*? The company may not have any local business. They may be a distribution center or do all their business overseas. That's okay. Because of Full Menu Marketing, you still have an opportunity to sell them some type of ticket product. Most likely this sale will simply transition into a Group Sale. It just takes you to ask a different group of questions. Here are the questions you would be asking:

**Q2.** "How many local *employees* do you have?"

**Q3.** "How do you recognize employees that go above and beyond and really help the company?"

**Q4.** "How often do you recognize your top employees?"

# *CHANGE OF DIRECTION*

## Notes on the Questions for Group Sales

**Q5**. This helps define how much the company spends on the program. It will help the salesperson make a price appropriate recommendation. It will also help determine if there is a committee or one person who decides the awards.

**Q6**. With multiple departments, each department could have one game a month to recognize a top employee. This would help build up the number of games needed each month.

**Q7**. If the company primarily recognizes the employees in a group setting, a nightly suite, party suite, or other larger one night hospitality event would be a better recommendation.

**Q8**. The salesperson will learn a lot about the primary employee outings and the budget for those outings. It will allow the salesperson to make a recommendation where the prospect could hold their company picnic or holiday party at a game.

**Q9**. The answer to this question will allow the salesperson to set up a group outing where the employees purchase tickets instead of the company footing the bill. The salesperson will need to give some examples of how it works at no risk to the prospect.

**Q5.** "What are the recognition awards?  How do you decide on the awards?"

**Q6.** "How many different departments do you have here?"

**Q7.** "Do you ever recognize and reward employees as a group or department?  What are those awards?"

**Q8.** "What do you do for a holiday party or summer picnic?"

**Q9.** "Do you provide the opportunity for employees to purchase tickets for events at a discount or with perks and benefits they couldn't get on their own?"

# *CHANGE OF DIRECTION*

## Notes on the Questions for Group Sales

**Q10**. Ideally, the salesperson has gleaned this information from the lobby plaques or office walls but it helps to have an explanation of how active the company is. A positive answer to this question would give ammunition to a charitable program using the team's tickets.

**Q11**. A charitable ticket program has tremendous flexibility to get the prospect to buy *something*. Set up varying tiers of donation so the company can pick a level. This is an almost last gasp to buy something if nothing else has worked or an easy add-on if the prospect has been exceptionally enthusiastic.

**Q10**. "What types of local community organizations is the company involved in?" (provide some examples like Boys and Girls Club, Scouts, etc.)

**Q11**. "Would you be interested in partnering with the team in a program where local underprivileged children have a chance to attend a Kangaroos game, compliments of your company? (If the CEO shows some interest, show an example of how this works…"(explain your team's charitable ticket program. If you don't have one, create one.)

# STUDY HELP

The following is to help you study the sales pitch and the objections. It's in script form. All the explanations from us are on the previous pages (except for a few 'Stage Directions that I feel obligated to do for your success.

# THE SALES PITCH

"Would you please hold this while we talk.  It's a tool we use in our business."

"We have a thing that we call silly putty tickets--remember silly putty, you can shape it, stretch it, mold it.   Well, we can shape and mold our tickets to your specific needs to help you increase your sales."

**(Q.1.)** "For instance, how many local salespeople do you have?" 5

**(Q.2.)** "How many key accounts does each salesperson have?"  5   ($25,000)

**(Q.3.)** "What size is an important account?"   125K

**(Q.4.)** "How important is new business to your salespeople?"

**(Q.5.)** "Do you have a strict plan that is designed to get new business every month?"

"It's always tough to get salespeople to focus on new business.

 By using our silly putty tickets, you can get them to *focus on new business,* and *you can keep track.*

 For example, the first step is to have each salesperson identify in writing to you which new prospects are key to them."

**(Q.6.)** "That wouldn't be difficult to do, would it?"

"Most of my clients have told me the key to building business from new prospects is for the salesperson to develop a good relationship with them, usually through constant contact.

A lot of times, to build that relationship, salespeople will use an out-of-the-office activity like golf or lunches.

Some of my clients have told me their problem with golf is that some people just may not be good golfers and it's almost more embarrassing to play than not. And, it's pretty expensive. And when was the last time you had a memorable chicken sandwich at lunch?

However, by using our silly putty tickets, you can get them to build these relationships and focus on new business, and you can keep track.

Here's how it works.

The salesperson calls a prospect who he has been working on for a little while. He says, 'How about joining me for the Kangaroos game next week? I've got the president's seats.'

This is <u>not</u> a situation of the salesperson just giving away the seats--it's the salesperson inviting the prospect *to go with him*. Now, the salesperson has the chance to do some real out-of-the-office bonding.

Remember, he wants to develop a relationship through constant contact. Giving the tickets away doesn't help build that relationship.

**(Q.7.)** "How effective do you think 2-3 hours at one of our Kangaroos games would be for building a relationship?"

*(If negative response):* "How do you mean?"

"Other companies thought that too, but look at how one of my clients have enjoyed success with our tickets..."

"You're exactly right, look at how one of my clients have enjoyed success with our tickets ...(Show Evidence Letter.)

"What could be even better when taking a prospect to a game is if you as the president or maybe your sales manager could go also."

**(Q.8.)** "Would you be willing to do that occasionally for the right account?"

**(Q.9.)** "Would it be asking too much of your salespeople to spend just one evening a month with a key prospect at one of our games?"

6 new pros

2 convert

$25,000 \times 2 = 50,000$

$5 \times 50,000 = 250,000$ potential NB per month

"Our season is about six months long. If each one of your salespeople took *just one key prospect a month to one of our games,* each salesperson would bring six new prospects a season."

**(Q.10.)** "Of those six prospects, how many do you think would end up as *customers?*"

"If each salesperson converted just ~~one~~ fewer prospect to become a new customer, that would be $ 25,000 (the avg. size of an important account from Q3) for each salesperson. With ___5___ (enter the number of salespeople from Q1) salespeople, that would be $ 125,000 in new business  (multiply the average size of an account by the number of local salespeople)."

**(Q.11.)** "Do you see how I arrived at this number?"

"You know, we've been talking about new business.  We might also consider your existing clients. After all, your competitor may be out there trying to build the same relationships with your clients."

**(Q.12.)** "Would it be asking too much to have your salespeople also spend just one evening with an existing client as well as one evening with a prospect?"

"To give each salesperson one game a month to take out a *prospect*, you would need ___5___ games a month."

**(Q.13.)** "Does that make sense to you?"

"You would need a similar amount of games per month for your salespeople to take *existing* clients out to the games."

"You would also need  105  games per month."

"You need a total of  105  games per month.  Now let's talk about which type of ticket would work best for you."

"Based on what you've told me, here's what I would suggest you do."

"Our best seating area is the Club Level.  With club seats, here is what you get…" (*outline the benefits of the club seats*). food, drinks, plasma, tablets

"The cost to have a planned, controlled, new business effort is really quite nominal for thereturn. For each one of your salespeople to take just one key prospect once a month and one current client a month, you would need  10  games per month or  60  games for the season."

(***Stage instruction***: *In our example, 5 salespeople would need 10 games per month or 60 games for the season. You should have a chart like the one in this manual on page 18.  Look at your chart and find the row with 5 salespeople.  You don't have to stumble around doing math, it's right there.*)

"The return on investment is substantial.  If each salesperson brought in only one piece of new business because of this focus on new business, your sales would increase by $125,000." ($25,000 x 5 = $125,000.)

"Because you need 60 games, I recommend four full season tickets. That would leave 10 games for your employees or more customers. Your costs for 4 season tickets is only $14,000."

"How happy do you think you'd be with those results by giving this plan a try? That decision would be worth at least $125,000 in new business to you and maybe up to $250,000 in new business."

"I can get this order in today and reserve you some prime seats."

**(Q.14.)** "Would you prefer the account in your name or the company's name?"

**(Stage instruction: PAUSE --- BE SILENT after asking Question 14.)**

# Handling Objections

## LET ME TALK TO MY PARTNER (or talk to someone else) Objection

CEO: "It sounds pretty good. Let me talk to my partner (wife or business manager or pet dog or whatever) and get back to you on this."

YOU: "I can understand wanting to talk to your partner. When do you think you'll do that?"

CEO: "Thursday (or whatever specific date)."

YOU: "Having looked at this program and looked at the new business potential, what will your recommendation be?"

CEO: "I would recommend it."

YOU: "What do you think your partner would be inclined to say?"

CEO: "I think he'd like it." (If the CEO gives you an objection here, ask "How do you mean?"

YOU: "Then why don't we do this? Let's sign you up today and we'll use our Opt-Out Clause. Here's how it works. You're meeting with your partner on Thursday. Well, I'll write next Monday's date at the top of the agreement. You have until that date to Opt-Out if you decide that this isn't for you. This way, you can get better seat locations, but if you and your partner decide that this isn't for you by next Monday, you just call me up and I'll cancel the order."

CEO: "I'm not sure. I really need to talk to him."

YOU: "We can still do the Opt Out. When you meet with your partner on Thursday (see above), and your partner doesn't like the $_____ in new revenue for a cost of $_____, then just call me and I'll cancel the deal."

CEO: "Looks pretty good. Let me talk to my salespeople and make sure they are into it and get back to you."

YOU: "When would you talk to your salespeople about this?"

CEO: "Thursday."

YOU: "Jim, you said earlier that it wouldn't be too much to ask of your salespeople to spend one night a month out with a key prospect, right?"

CEO: "I think it's reasonable."

YOU: "And, you said you thought Big City Kangaroos games were a good place to develop relationships and there was a potential of _____ in new business, right?"

CEO: "Sure."

YOU: "Then with all due respect to your salespeople, why let them even vote on it? Why let them vote on $125,000 of new revenue for your company? If you think this will work and you think they have to spend just one evening a month out with a prospect, and generate $125,000 to $250,000 in new business, what's there to vote on? *What if they voted no?* I had a client last year who was concerned about whether his salespeople would use the tickets. Here's how well it worked for him."

**(STAGE DIRECTIONS: Hand a testimonial letter to the CEO.)** (To see what to say see following page).

YOU: (when CEO looks up from the letter) "Why don't we do this? Let's sign you up today and we'll use our Opt-Out Clause. Here's how it works. You're meeting with your salespeople on Thursday (see above). Well, I'll write next

Monday's date at the top of the agreement. You have until that date to Opt-Out if you decide that this isn't for you. This way, you can get better seat locations, but if your sales staff really fights you on this, by next Monday, just call me up and I'll cancel the order. Can I reserve those seats today?"

**BE SILENT AND LET THE PROSPECT SPEAK NEXT**

## COST TOO MUCH objection

YOU: "How do you mean?"

CEO: "Well, we've had a tough year and cut some budgets so I have to be smart on expenses" (or some other expanded explanation).

YOU: "I can understand that. (pause) You know, think about it this way. You said yourself that you thought you could generate $ _____ in new business for a pretty reasonable cost of $ _____ . That sounds like a pretty smart move on your part. What is it here that is really causing you to hesitate?"

## BE SILENT AND LET THE PROSPECT SPEAK NEXT

**(STAGE DIRECTIONS**: If the prospect really continues to persist that it is indeed a cost issue, you don't want to become pushy. It's okay to downsell them to make them more comfortable with the purchase. Your goal is to make a sale.)

YOU: "What would you be more comfortable with?"

**(STAGE DIRECTIONS: Whatever figure he gives you, it's probably the low figure. Come up with a package that is lower than your original figure but a little higher than his.)**

YOU: "Within that price range I think this could work for you (cut the original recommendation down with either a cheaper priced ticket or fewer games).

"With this plan, you can still get really good seat locations and pretty close to the right number of games. If this works the way we both think it will, you can always add games or upgrade your seats during the season. Will this work for you?"

## NONE OF MY CLIENTS ARE HOCKEY/BASEBALL/BASKETBALL FANS Objection
## Or
## LET ME TALK TO A FEW CLIENTS TO SEE IF THEY ARE INTERESTED Objection

YOU: "How do you mean?"

CEO: (Some additional explanation)

YOU: "That makes sense to think about your clients. Let's really think about this though. This program really is designed to get *new* business. You said earlier that our games would be an effective place to build relationships, right? Well, prospects might not be fans of our team, but most like to see the biggest stars of the league at some of our biggest and best sold out games. This works for getting new business and it will work for most of your clients.

I can take your order right now and get this new business program going."

## BE SILENT AND LET THE PROSPECT SPEAK NEXT

---

**I'll JUST BUY THE GOOD GAMES
FROM STUB HUB** Objection

---

CEO: "I'll just buy the good games from Stub Hub."

YOU: "I can understand how easy it is to buy from StubHub. However, StubHub has some weaknesses for businesses:

1. "You can't really plan in advance with a controlled new business strategy.

2. "You never really know how much you'll pay for tickets and more importantly, whether you can get decent seats.

3. "You also don't get access to the other features and benefits of being a ticket package buyer with the team.

"What is it that is really causing you to hesitate here?"

---
**I CAN'T SEE THIS WORKING** objection
---

CEO: "I just can't see this working…"

YOU: "I can understand that this sounds crazy that you can get all this new business by going to games. But, IT DOES WORK. And, what is your risk? It's only about $14,000. That's not much of a gamble—$14,000 to get $125,000, maybe $250,000. What if it isn't as effective as I say it is? What if it's only 75% effective? That would mean you would get over $90,000 in new business for a $14,000 investment. Plus you'll have a lot of fun at our games.   Would it be all right if I placed your order today?"

## LET ME THINK ABOUT IT Objection

CEO: "I'd like to think about it."

YOU: "I can understand that. If you took some time to think about it—maybe even thinking about it walking some beach—and you thought about the $_____ in new sales and the $_____ in cost, do you think you would be *inclined* to do it?"

(If the answer is *yes* or *probably*, say, "Well, then, why don't we just do it? You'll really be pleased with the results.")

(If the answer is *no* or *probably not*, ask why. "Really? You'd be getting $_____ in new revenue and it cost only $_____. What is it that's really causing you to hesitate here?")

(You'll probably get a real objection. Now you can handle the objection directly.)

## TO THOSE WHO HESITATE

CEO: (Hesitating)

YOU: "Let me tell you about another CEO that was in the same position as you and he followed this plan and decided to give it a try. Take a look at these numbers..."

**(Hand the prospect another Endorsement Letter and be quiet while the CEO reads it.)**

YOU: "How happy do you think he is that he gave this plan a try? That decision was worth $100,000 in new business to him. Let me get this order in today. Don't worry about a thing, I'll take care of all the details..."

## MAKING THE DECISION

**(Stage direction:  You can use this anytime while handling objections.)**

YOU:  "Let's take a look at this. . .the pros and the cons.

(Take out a blank piece of paper for this.  Draw a line vertically down the middle.  Write 'Pros' in the upper left and 'Cons' in the upper right.)

Let's put down the amount of new business in the left hand column..." **(Stage direction: hand write the new business number on your chart.)**

YOU:  "Of that new business you would get, is it business that you can *renew*?  If so, what percent do you think you could renew?"  **(Stage direction:  based on the answer, hand write that number on your chart.)**

YOU: "That's $225,000 in new business, and that's if your salespeople convert only one in six of their prospects. Now let's look at the Cons."

YOU:  "What would be the first 'reason against'?"

YOU: "You might say expense. Let me write down $14,400."

**(Stage direction: hand write the cost of the ticket package you're recommending.)**

YOU: "Anything else?"

CEO: "I don't know how effective this would be."

**(Stage direction: hand write that objection onto the Reasons Against column. You then handle that objection like we have outlined in this Handbook.)**

YOU: "Let's take a look at this. It looks like a pretty easy decision. You get $225,000 in new revenue at a cost of $14,000. Let me get your order in today…"

## GETTING THE FOLLOW-UP MEETING

**STAGE INSTRUCTION: Every meeting doesn't end in a yes or no answer. There are times when follow up is needed. You should never settle for a follow-up phone call. Usually that ends up becoming a lot of chasing of the CEO to get a final yes or no answer. It's better to get the follow-up meeting when you're already meeting with the CEO. Getting the follow-up meeting could go like this:**

CEO: "I'm not sure about this and have to talk to a few people first. Give me a call next week and I'll let you know."

YOU: "I can understand that. I am actually going to be right down the street at _____ (insert company) for a meeting at 10:00am on Tuesday. Would it be okay to stop by here at 9:30am to answer any new questions or get this wrapped up?"

**STAGE DIRECTIONS: The salesperson should be reaching in to their bag for an appointment book or their cell phone for a calendar. This will make it seem more 'official' that they are going to be back in the area.**

CEO: (will give you a yes/no answer or another date)

**STAGE DIRECTIONS: Once the CEO says *yes*, the salesperson should mark the date down on either their phone calendar or in their appointment book. Don't just write it on a sheet of paper.**

YOU: "Great, I've got down that I will see you next Tuesday at 9:30am. Does that work for you?"

## WHAT IF THEY DON'T HAVE ANY LOCAL SALESPEOPLE?

**Q1 (Alternative Direction) STAGE INSTRUCTIONS:** Remember the first question of this presentation, "How many local salespeople do you have?" Well, here's what you say when the answer is *zero*. The company may not have any local business. They may be a distribution center or do all their business overseas. That's okay. Because of Full Menu Marketing, you still have an opportunity to sell them some type of ticket product. Most likely this sale will simply transition into a Group Sale. You just ask a different group of questions. Here are the questions you would be asking:

**Q2.** "How many local *employees* do you have?"

**Q3.** "How do you recognize employees that go above and beyond and really help the company?"

**Q4.** "How often do you recognize your top employees?"

**Q5.** "What are the recognition awards? How do you decide on the awards?"

**Q6.** "How many different departments do you have here?"

**Q7**. "Do you ever recognize and reward employees as a group or department? What are those awards?"

**Q8**. "What do you do for a holiday party or summer picnic?"

**Q9**. "Do you provide the opportunity for employees to purchase tickets for events at a discount or with perks and benefits they couldn't get on their own?"

**Q10**. "What types of local community organizations is the company involved in? (provide some examples like Boys and Girls Club, Scouts, etc.)"

**Q11**. "Would you be interested in partnering with the team in a program where local underprivileged children have a chance to attend a Kangaroos game, compliments of your company? (If the CEO shows some interest) Let me give you an example of how this works…."(explain your team's charitable ticket program. If you don't have one, create one.)

# WHAT'S INSIDE *THE ULTIMATE TOOLKIT*

1. **Selling the Last Seat: Strategy & Tactics *Playbook*.** This is essential to selling out games. You need to have a specific philosophy and strategy to sell out games. Read and study this first. There are three volumes.

## *VOLUME I*

# Volume II

*season tickets.*

## Volume III

*purchasing a suite.*

2. **Ticket Sales Manager's Bible**.   A key player in implementing your sellout strategy is your Ticket Sales Manager.  That person needs to understand and embrace the sellout

philosophy and strategy as much as you do. This book was written specifically for the Ticket Sales Manager to help that person implement the sellout strategy and tactics.

## CONTENTS

3. **Ticket Sales Manager's Boot Camp Manual**. We're huge believers in serious training of your ticket sales people. Part of the training we recommend is a Ticket Sales Boot

Camp.  This workbook gives your Ticket Sales Manager step-by-step guidelines to running a highly effective Boot Camp.

## CONTENTS

4. **Getting the Sale Handbook**. Each salesperson that attends your Boot Camp gets this tutorial. There's 50 pages on what to specifically say during a sales pitch and how to answer various objections.

5. **Getting the Appointment Handbook**. Each salesperson that attends your Boot Camp gets this tutorial on how to make appointments with any CEO. There are 36 pages on what to specifically say to get eyeball-to-eyeball appointments.

6. **Group Sales Manager's Bible**. Group sales are important in the sellout strategy. This book was written specifically for the Group Sales Manager, featuring the day-to-day responsibilities in helping achieve more sellouts.

# CONTENTS

7. **Group Sales Manager's Boot Camp Planning Guide.** Yes, there is a separate Boot Camp for group sales. This is the guide the Group Sales Manager can use to have a highly effective boot camp.

## CONTENTS

8. **Group Salesperson's Handbook**. Each group salesperson that attends the Group Sales Boot Camp gets this tutorial. 39 pages on who specifically to call on at various organizations, what to say and how to answer objections.

9. **Inside Sales Manager's Boot Camp Guide.** Telemarketing is important, particularly for individual sales. Most teams provide very little training (which includes no training

or just tossing a list to the telemarketer.) We know, however, that training clearly ramps up productivity. In this Boot Camp Guide, the Inside Sales Manager will have everything that is needed to quickly boost sales.

## CONTENTS

10. **Inside Salesperson's Handbook**. Many of a team's telemarketers are young and don't have a lot of experience. They need to be trained to handle three different types of sales calls.

**Part 1**: **Follow up calls to renewing season ticketholders**. The Handbook gives each telemarketer the tools to improve the renewal rate of the season ticket accounts. The Handbook walks through key steps to handling objections and provide effective answers to objections.

**Part 2: Calls to prospective new buyers**. The Handbook gives specific instruction on how to make follow up calls to people that already have an interest in the team and have already come to some of the team's games. The Handbook shows the Inside Sales rep how to ask the right questions, handle objections and close sales.

**Part 3: Handling in-bound calls from prospective buyers.** Your team will send out letters and emails and run ads promoting your ticket packages. Fans will call in to ask questions. We give your telemarketers the keys to answering those questions, asking additional questions and closing sales.

11. **President's Ticket Sales Bible.** Even if the President isn't a ticket sales expert, they still need to pay attention to tickets. This booklet was specifically written for the team president to know what to look for, what questions to ask and how to help the team's ticket sales experts succeed.

12. **Video: Ticket Sales Pitch**. What does a perfect ticket sales pitch to a CEO look like? Here it is. Use this as a benchmark for your salespeople to achieve.

13. **Video: Group Sales Pitch**. How about a perfect group sales pitch? Here's a copy. Use this as a benchmark for your group salespeople to achieve.

14. **Assistance as Close as the Internet**. Our website, **www.theultimatetoolkit.com**, was created as another tool specifically for marketers that have purchased our *Toolkit*. On this website, we have ads that worked for us. We have forms that we have used. We have renewal letters that have worked for us. All of this you can download, tweak, and use. Here are some of the things you can download from www.theultimatetoolkit.com:

**ADS**

Here are a bunch of ads that I wrote. All of them achieved at least a $4-to-$1 ratio (revenue to cost) except one. Spoiler alert: the one ad that didn't pull is in the document below titled 'Alas.'

7 game elf ad dmn.pdf
2008 all you can eat baseball 3x7.pdf
7G Secret Spice2.pdf
All You Can Eat2.pdf
Best seat promise$15.jpg
Best seat promise$15.pdf
Daddy-daughter3.pdf
DMN Heaven small ad.pdf
Family math McDonalds.pdf
Free prize inside2.pdf
FriscoFF May 18.pdf
FRR Eating with Santa Plan A.pdf
Go to fewer games.pdf
Here or your backyard2.pdf
I hire elves 3.pdf
I'll buy you dinner FINAL.pdf
I'm no rocket scientist, 4.19.pdf
IsThisHeaven.pdf
Magic Waters 3 col. x 10.pdf
Manhattan version2.pdf
My husband is so smart (2).pdf

New York Daily News wrap FINAL.pdf
No video games here.pdf
SWB_ChampD_Whoa.pdf
why not buy later 2.pdf
You get the best deal $9 version.pdf

## RENEWAL LETTERS

The most important mailing of the year.

Renewal Introduction.pdf
First Renewal Letter Example for Ticket Package Buyers.pdf
Last Gasp Renewal Letter.pdf
Renewal Picture books.JPG
Ticket Delivery Cooler Bag.JPG
Renewal Puzzle.JPG
Renewal Relocation Form.pdf
Second Renewal Letter Example.pdf
Ticket Package Invoice Example.pdf

## TICKET SALES LETTERS

These letters range from our $3 letter that helps get an appointment with a big-company CEO to our series of Dormant Letters.

$3 and a cup of coffee.doc
Dormant Letter _1 - Introduction.doc
Dormant Letter _2 Personal Sweepstakes.doc
Dormant _3 -Interesting stuff.doc
Dormant Letter _4.doc

## BOOT CAMP: OUTSIDE SALES

Getting the Appointment Telechart cards.ppt
Getting the Appointment Handbook.pdf
Getting the Appointment slides.ppt

Salesperson's copy of Getting the Sale Handbook.pdf
Salesperson's copy of THE SALES PITCH.doc
Outside Sales Pitch Slides.ppt
Sales Pitch to Corporations Video (download)
test questions _1.doc
test questions _2.doc
test questions _3.doc

## BOOT CAMP: GROUP SALES

Group Salesperson's Handbook - Final.pdf
Group Training Slides - Final.ppt
Group Sales Marketing Collateral Introduction.pdf
Group Catalog Example.pdf
Group Sales Direct Mail Example - School Principals.pdf

Nightly Rental Suite one sheet.pdf
Party Deck Group One-sheet.pdf
Party Deck Group One-sheet.pdf

The Perfect Group Sales Pitch Video (download)

## BOOT CAMP: INSIDE SALES

Inside Sales Training Slides.ppt
Inside Salesperson's Handbook.pdf
Generic Phone Log.doc
Individuals Database Example.xls

## WHO TO CALL ON

Your Outside Salespeople are going to call on executives from a lot of different industries. To help you salespeople call on the right person at a company—and why that executive should buy tickets for the company—we've done a series of 'Industry Reports.' These reports will help your salespeople on better understanding of the ticket needs for each industry.

Industry Introduction.pdf
Accounting Firms.pdf
Banks.pdf
Construction Industry.pdf

Commercial Real Estate.pdf
Doctors and Dentists.pdf
Financial Services _ Brokers.pdf
Food and Beverage Manufacturers.pdf
Food Service Brokers and Distributors.pdf
Hospitals.pdf
Hotels.pdf
Law Firms.pdf
Printing Companies.pdf
Professional Services.pdf
Retailers.pdf

## ONE-SHEET LEAVE BEHINDS

7-Game Pinstripe Plan.pdf
7-Game One-Sheet Update.pdf
21-game Pinstripe.pdf
Club Seats One Sheet.pdf
Field Seats One Sheet.pdf

## REPORTS

Here are reports that you can use to keep track of your team's progress with ticket sales. A key report is Outside Sales Calls and Appointments. If your salespeople are making an adequate number of appointments, your team will be making its sales goals.
Outside Sales Calls and Appointments.xls

Direct Mail Tracking Report.xls
Print Ad Tracker.xls
Summary Ticket Activity Report.xls
Renewal Report.xls
Daily New Sales Report.xls